A Sojourn With A Smile

Michael Gordon Dickson

Copyright © 2015 Michael Gordon Dickson

All rights reserved.

ISBN:1519311818
ISBN-13:9781519311818

DEDICATION

TO

JANET

TABLE OF CONTENTS

No News Tonight..................................9
Like Father Like Son..........................12
In Search of Wisdom.........................14
Flat Pack..17
All That Passed Me By......................20
Your Name is George........................22
For Heaven's Sake.............................25
Honey Bee..27
Two of Diamonds..............................29
I Have Days......................................32
When Boys and Girls Come Out to Play.....34
The Loveliest of All...........................36
Lest I Forget.....................................38
Fair Share...42
These Grapes Are Rather Nice.........45
Epitaph...47
Pick Up the Pieces............................49
When You Were Very Small..............51
Welcome to Purgatory......................55
If I Had a Penny................................58

Old Adversaries................61
He Who Knows................64
All As One................67
On the First Day of Lent................69
More or Less................72
Garden Censor................75
Human Interaction................78
After Delivery................82
Litterbug................84
The Fault Finding Society................88
Addiction................91
Happy Whatever................94
Metamorphosis................96
Without Adversity................99
So Last Century................101
Your Fellow Servant................103
It's a Beautiful Day................105
It's Your World Now................107
As You Find Them................110
Something Will Happen................112
Hedgehog Crossing................114
The Bank Note................116
No Good Will................120
Bittersweet................123

How Deep a Heart	126
Colour Co-ordination	128
The Psychiatrist	131
The Short Straw	134
Recycled Rib	138
Humbug	141
I Always Tried	144
If I Can Help	147
Empty Handed	149
Wear It With Pride	152
Your Captain Speaking	154
Flood Alert	158
Just As Green	161
Missing Stethoscope	163
Family Tree	167
Prayer For The Departed	169
Hen or Egg	171
The Hypochondriologist	174
Passing Strangers	177
The Customer is Always Right	179
Forgiveness	183
Fatal Accident	185
Multitude of Greys	188

NO NEWS TONIGHT

"There is no news tonight
We are sorry to say.
Our nightly bulletin
Is less than paper thin
Nothing newsworthy has occurred today.

There have been no earthquakes
There have been no hurricanes
No wars have been declared
No innocents were massacred
And there were no reports of any missing planes.

No bombs were exploded
To leave mothers' tear-stained faces
And there was no adultery
Concerning a celebrity
And there was no corruption in high places.

No species became extinct
No borders were encroached

No new death virus was detected
No new health plan was rejected
And in Africa, no elephant was poached.

No-one was lost at sea
No homes were set alight
No logging company
Felled one rainforest tree
No homeless person slept out in the cold last night.

There were no crimes committed
Police reported none at all.
No murderer escaped
No woman was raped
And the Samaritans did not receive a call.

No politician told a lie
No spin doctors were used
No starving child died in despair
No care home gave no care
And there was not one child who was abused."

The presenter says, "Good night"

And throws down his blank news sheets
He leaves the studio
Then sees out of the window
That thousands are dancing in the streets.

LIKE FATHER, LIKE SON

I wasn't slow to get started.
I discovered on an early day
That if I shook the pram and I shrieked
What I wanted, I'd get right away.

Sometimes I would be reprimanded
Because of the mood I was in
Then I'd scream and I'd scream and I'd scream
And I'd kick my dad on his shin.

I poisoned my mother's goldfish.
My gran's zimmer I hid in the shed
And I found a big slug in the garden
And put it in mum and dad's bed.

At school, they all had lunch boxes,
The only good reason to go.
I had my fill of their crisps and chocolate
While they all searched high and low.

My teacher had a nervous breakdown.
She blamed me for her funny turns.
When she left the classroom in tears
I filled up her handbag with worms.

Then I was sent to the headmaster.
He said, "You're not what this school requires."
I found his car in the car park
And I let down all of his tyres.

When I left school I was successful
For nobody stood in my way
And I became head of department
With appropriate deference each day.

Soon I took myself a wife,
Submissively quiet who obeyed
And I enjoyed my just rewards
King of all that I surveyed.

But then I had a child of my own
And I soon had my fill of that
I simply don't know where he came from,
For he is a horrible brat.

IN SEARCH OF WISDOM

Everyday he sat outside his humble shack
Gazing vacantly into empty space
And no-one might ever tell what he was thinking
From his expressionless and deeply wrinkled face.

Hesitantly the boy approached the old man
And said, "Sir, my teacher said that it is true
That the older someone gets, the more wisdom that they have
And I wondered then if I might learn from you?"

The old man sat in silence, staring at the boy
Then in irritation shook his head
And in monotone of voice, he began to speak
And the boy listened, alert to what he said.

"Don't put your hand in boiling water

Don't pick on bigger men to fight,
Remember every second driver
Who signals left, will then turn right.

When you play with gas and fire,
Don't play with both at the same time.
Never trust a politician
Don't picnic on a railway line.

Borrow money from amnesiacs
Don't argue with a gun,
Say the cheque is in the post
Grab sweets from strangers and then run.

Don't let a drunken barber
Ever cut your hair.
Volunteer for nothing,
Don't take honey from a bear.

Clean up your house every July,
Stay in bed on Christmas day
Ignore people at your door
Pretty soon, they'll go away."

Disappointedly, the boy then duly thanked him
Then he turned and made to walk away
But slowly the old man's expression softened
And he gently called upon the boy to stay.

And he said, "Son, I have made light of what you asked me,
I did not take you seriously from the start.
Let me give you the only wisdom that I own
And this time, what I say is from the heart.

When you grow up and find somebody loves you
Be sure that she is treasured every day.
Be certain not to ever take that love for granted
Or like me, you'll be alone when old and grey."

FLAT PACK

Congratulations on making a fine choice,
Manufactured in the Far East for your home.
This piece you have selected
In quickest time will be erected
And it will make you proud to call your own.

Unpack the box and be laying items out.
There is no requirement for a drill
But have screwdriver and a hammer,
A set square and a spanner
And you may wish to take anti-depressant pill.

Now take the shelf marked "zx" on the instructions
And hold it next to "ql" on one side.
In screw holes "a" to "f" then use
One inch brass head screws
(Please note that one inch brass head screws are not supplied.)

Place piece "f65" next to back panel v94
And match up with screw holes one to nine.
Should this a problem give
Take a sedative
And borrow drill if screw holes don't align.

Should brackets 2 and 6 have been omitted,
Then the movement of the drawer may be slack
But this is elemental
For the drawer is not essential
And it will leave a useful space for bric-a-brac.

Now put the runners next to "c"
And the crossbar next to "e"
And align the shelves with side-panels "j4"
Then screw the framework on the base
Make sure the back plate is in place
Now all that is remaining is the door.

Then be needing three friends to help stand it
But be advising that their hands may need protecting,
Although the screws supplied are right,
If they are screwed in too tight,
It can be that the screw points are projecting.

If the model that you chose is "Panama"
Perhaps there may be problem with the door.
Once dispatched, we realised
The door may be oversized
Take ten centimetres off it with a saw.

In the unlikely chance that you may have a problem,
We are here to help in your duress.
Simply call back at the store
Where you purchased this before
And feel free to take advantage
Of our manageress.

ALL THAT PASSED ME BY

I've never owned a yacht
With a five man crew,
I've never been a millionaire
I've never been to Kathmandu.

I've never drunk vintage champagne
Never attended gala nights
I've never owned a Rolex watch
I've never seen my name in lights.

I've never been on a world cruise
The Taj Mahal I've never seen
I've never eaten caviare
I've never met the queen.

I've never dined at Claridges
I've never had too much to spend
I've never heard a nightingale
I never found my rainbow's end.

But…..I've never needed chemotherapy

I've never been in an earthquake
I never have been bankrupt
Never been bitten by a snake.

I've never failed to have a roof
I've never fallen from a height
I've never been gripped by addiction
I've never lost my sight.

I've never slept in a shop doorway
With no blanket reconciled,
I've never had an empty larder
I've never mourned a stillborn child.

I've never been wrongly convicted
I've never needed a brain scan
I've never had to go to war
I've never had to kill a man.

For that which failed to come my way
There were times I'd question why,
Instead of being truly thankful
For all that passed me by.

YOUR NAME IS GEORGE

On the first day that she failed to recognise him
It was as though an arrow pierced his heart.
Later he would weep
With a pain that hurt so deep
For a son and mother now were torn apart.

Always he'd make time to go to see her
Knowing the outcome would ever be the same.
They would talk awhile
Then she would give a vague smile
And ask the question he would dread, "What is your name?"

And each time that she asked the question
It would cut right through him like a knife
For she no longer knew
Who she was talking to,
The son she'd carried and to whom had given life.

They said to him, "Why don't you end these visits
For each time you go, you are torn apart?"
But he just smiled and said
My visits must go ahead
For it was she who taught me, "Follow your heart."

Then came the day that he always knew would come
And he knelt beside her bed with his goodbyes.
Strangely, he felt serene
Remembering how she had once been
But left the care home with tears in his eyes.

Once the funeral had duly passed,
One more duty he had to do next day.
Offers to help, he spurned
And to the care home he returned
To take all her belongings away.

Then as he was departing from her room,
Beneath her pillow, a scrap of paper caught his view.
He leaned over the bed

And picked it up and read,
"Your name is George and I always will love you."

FOR HEAVEN'S SAKE

St. Peter shook his head and said, "I'm sorry,
The paperwork says that you can't come in.
The story of your life makes dismal reading...
An existence of hypocrisy and sin."

I said, "Are you aware to whom you're speaking?
For heaven's sake, I am a most important man!
I rose to the peak of my profession
Unlike for example, Jim McCann.

Next you'll be telling me that he's been granted entry
While you are turning a high court judge away.
It was my privilege on many an occasion
To sentence such a man to prison stay."

"Indeed Mr. Mc.Cann died only yesterday
And on this spot he knelt on bended knee
For in good works for many years he had repented

And in forgiveness, he was granted entry."

I said, "What kind of business are you running
When you dare to speak to me in such a tone
While you welcome in the likes of Jim Mc.Cann?"
Then I stopped as Peter answered his phone.

He spoke awhile and then turned back to me,
"Mr. Mc.Cann on your behalf has interceded,
On his own, he occupies a double room
And says he'd welcome you to share should it be needed."

I said, "You people are way beyond belief
If you expect a dignitary such as me
To live in the company of a petty criminal
And be disgusted for all eternity!"

And as the phone rang once again, I told him
"If you know what's good for you, plead my case well."
He turned and said, "It's the managing director,
I am instructed to advise you...go to hell."

HONEYBEE

When flowers begin to bloom
To signify springtime
Her lifetime work begins
And she flies in a bee-line.
She finds the early bluebells
In tepid sunshine in the wood
And nothing now will stop her working
For her species greater good.
The flowers bid her welcome,
Their scent and colour woo her
Brushed with pollen, drawing nectar,
She is their genetic courier.
Then she flies back and forth
Up to two miles each way
From tempting blossoms to her hive
To bring the nectar home each day.
There, she will dance the nectar dance,
Her choreography will show
Her sisters, flower directions
Where tomorrow they should go.
Then summer warms the air

Seductive petals make display
And now from dawn to dusk
She works each second of the day.
And the honeycomb is growing
Back home in the hive
But winter nights are long
It must grow more that they survive.
She would not call fatigue an issue
If she but had vocabulary
For the individual is lesser
Than all of her colony.
And as the summer sun grows weaker
At the roadside you may see
The black and gold striped dying form
Of an exhausted honeybee.
But she dies in satisfaction.
She did what she had to do.
To mother nature she was loyal,
Her hive will see the winter through.
Would that man might learn a lesson
For from the honey bee he could,
That he might live his life according to
His species greater good.

TWO OF DIAMONDS

When I was dealt out of the pack
I was quick to realise
The two of Diamonds is a lowly card
Which no player would prize.

Although I tried to play the game
I soon found to my cost,
All the other cards were better
And every trick I lost.

The Jack of Spades kept laughing
And he said to my face,
"Why don't you get back in the box?
You're just a waste of space."

Then King of Hearts and Queen of Clubs
Said, "You are bottom of the list.
Just get back in the box
You won't even be missed."

So I crawled back in the box

To find the Joker there.
I told him to let me be
And I cried in my despair.

But soon he put an arm around me
And said, "Get out there and kick lumps.
Little two this is your moment
Diamonds are nominated trumps."

Then he pushed me from the box
Straight back into play
And I took the Jack of Spades
Which took my breath away.

I beat the King and Queen of Hearts
I played the ten of Clubs and won.
The King of Diamonds stood and shouted,
"You can do this little one."

Then last was the Ace of Spades,
The deadliest card in name.
I was stunned to beat him
And to find I'd won the game.

All the Diamonds clustered round me

And patted me upon the back.
They said, "Today you are our champion,
The best card in the pack."

So if you're small and insignificant,
Don't be down in the dumps
For everyone will have their day
When they can come up trumps.

I HAVE DAYS

I have days this world lies heavy on my shoulders
When what I see of man's affairs discomforts me
And to be here is not a place that I might choose
But I know of no other place
That I might be.

I have days the passing years have taken liberties
With my sinews and my muscles and my veins
And they whisper that it may be I am mortal
And these are the days
It always rains.

I have days that I look back on past successes,
Seeming important then but meaning little now
For on the stage of personal achievement
I have delivered my last line
And made my bow.

I have days life is extinguished of all meaning
And it seems I walk a treadmill pointlessly

Then I must light the blue touchpaper of my spirit
And permit its tiny flame
To strengthen me.

Yet I have days my upturned face is bathed in sunlight
And every hour is negative of care
Then I walk with the lightest of all footsteps
And I mellow to the birdsong
In the air.

There will be many do not see the hours of twilight
For the setting sun is taken from their gaze.
Yet once again I see the dawn is softly breaking
And I bow my head in thanks
That I have days.

BOYS AND GIRLS COME OUT TO PLAY

When boys and girls come out to play
All the problems begin that day
For once the boys discard their toys,
That's the time that boys will be boys.

Girls were playing a different game
Where dolls and babies were much the same
But they can put their dolls away
When boys and girls come out to play.

Then boys exchange skate boards and kites
For nappy changing and sleepless nights
And girls sometimes regret the day
When boys and girls came out to play.

For dolls are now the real thing
And real ones need lots of upbringing
And girls must watch as they work away
That boys don't go back out to play.

Yet mother nature cares not one bit
What mums and dads will make of it,
Her duty was done upon the day
That boys and girls came out to play.

But if they strive for years to come
Playing less games and having less fun,
They will be wiser and they will bid
To counsel their brood not to do what they did.

Then they will be in a nervous state
As they re-open their garden gate
For once again has arrived the day
When boys and girls come out to play.

THE LOVELIEST OF ALL

Rose, it has been too long
Since we had to part
But as I make your re-acquaintance,
Once more, you touch my heart.

In your absence I grew weak
And was distracted for a while
By the daintiness of Marigold
And her sunny, golden smile.

I could have been seduced by Violet
Though old-fashioned and petite,
There was no shortage of admirers
Gathered round her feet.

Then there was Poppy, brash and sultry,
A hot, flamenco queen
Who vied for my affection
When she burst upon the scene.

Next came Lily, cool and regal
Who made my senses soar
With her majesty of presence
And the enticing scent she wore.

In her train there followed Iris,
Exotic and fragile.
I would have had her linger
But she would only stay awhile.

I was much taken with Angelica
And drawn to Jasmine too.
How could I not admire Veronica
While I waited for you?

Now I behold your bounteous vision
And to your perfume, I enthral.
There are but none to be your equal,
You are the loveliest of all.

So forgive me my flirtations
Every ounce of me implores.
I am but a humble gardener
But Rose, my heart is yours.

LEST I FORGET

Lest I forget, I will make use of rubber bands
And slip them on my wrists over both hands
Then when I see them, I am sure to remember
But that means that I must find some rubber bands.

I believe that I had some in my toolbox
But in the garden shed, the box is gone.
It can't be stolen for the door is always locked.
Maybe I lent the toolbox out to John?

Now it's coming back to me quite clearly,
I remember lending the toolbox to John.
I recall him standing asking in my doorway
Or was that his older brother Ron?

No matter, I'll give John a call
And I'll ask him if he will take a look
In case he had forgotten to return it.
So I'll call him, when I find the telephone book.

The book has vanished from where it should be.
Now I feel my head is getting sore.
For an hour I ransack all the house,
Until I find it in the cutlery drawer.

At last I can sit down to call up John
If to recall his surname, I am able.
I slump down with the book on my settee.
Why is my mobile missing from the coffee table?

This time I will not search all of the house.
I will stay quite calm and will not lose it.
I will quietly get on with household jobs
While I consider where I last did use it.

So I hoover and I do the washing up
Thinking when I used it last, where had I been?
Then as I unload the laundry in the basket
I find it waterlogged in the washing machine.

I cannot find the microwave instructions
So I put the cellphone into a chipped cup.
I believe they said that it could dry things out
But they were lying for the microwave blew up.

Now thanks to treacherous microwave makers,
I am left without a phone today
So I will take a walk and go and visit John
For he only lives two blocks away.

His wife opens the door and looks severe
And says,"I thought that you considered John as friend,
Yet yesterday at his funeral service,
I couldn't help but notice you did not attend?"

I muttered and I mumbled in confusion
My self esteem was now a dying ember,
I had been sure there was a niggle on my mind,
Something important that I had to remember.

Then she begins to shake and wring her hands
And as she weeps, I turn numb inside
So I decide it's best that I don't ask her
If he'd mentioned a toolbox before he died.

I go home and I climb through the window
Since I find that I don't have my keys.
Once again I search the house from top to bottom

Until I find them in the fridge beside the cheese.

Now the nights are drawing in and growing cold
And today I've had too many shocks and traumas.,
I'm miserable and tired and depressed.
I think I'll take out my winter pyjamas.

Aha! Bingo and eureka, hallelujah!
Here they are in my bedside bottom drawer!
Rubber bands on top of my pyjamas.
Now what was it that I wanted them for?

FAIR SHARE

The cards were dealt before I knew
The rules that I had to play to
I left them lying, face down and unturned
But soon the knowledge grew
Of what I had to do,
I picked up my hand
And then I learned.

I played the best I could
Some deals were bad and some were good
But now and then there was a hand that made
me smile.
Then there would come a round
That I would win hands down
But that occurred only once in a while.

Time and again would come a day
When there were no cards I could play
For I could not reverse the run that I was in
Then I would have to try

Not to cast a jealous eye
At the player who always
Seemed to win.

For this game did not seem to yield
A level playing field
From the moment that the first deal had begun,
Some hands would always lack
The aces in the pack
While trump cards fell into
The hands of some.

Then at the dealer's command,
I played my last hand
Then to the dealer I laid my soul bare
And as I reassessed the game
Just ended in my name,
I told him I had thought
The game unfair.

And I explained to him
That I had tried so hard to win
But with the cards I had been given, felt betrayed.
Then the dealer shook his head

And he gently said
That the game was more about the way
One played.

He said, "You must understand
That what I give you in one hand
In the next hand I give to another player
And what appears a random game
Levels in each entrant's name
And I always gave you
Your fair share."

THESE GRAPES ARE RATHER NICE

I was walking past the hospital
With a few minutes to kill
And thought I'd come to cheer you up,
Since I heard that you were ill.

So let me sit and look you over.
Good lord! It isn't hard to tell
Why you're languishing in here,
For you look seriously unwell.

You must excuse me yawning.
I've been on the go since dawn.
You don't know how lucky you are
To lie there and be waited on.

No wonder there's infection here
And most people leave here dead.
Have you seen all the dust
Underneath your bed?

So you've been desperately unlucky

To have your house burgled twice
While you've been in hospital.
These grapes are rather nice.

You know, they tell you they are clean.
They must take us for mugs.
When I met your son last week
I'm sure he was back on drugs.

I saw your wife the other day
With Alexander Spector.
He's such a touchy-feely man
For a funeral director.

You're going to have another visitor
For I heard Nurse O'Hara say
They've called the priest to come to see you
And they insist he comes today.

I'll come again to cheer you
Depending on what time I've got,
So goodbye, I'll see you soon
But then again, maybe I'll not.

EPITAPH

Here lies Maurice Shuttlecock
A pastor of this town
Once a familiar figure
In white collar and black gown.

 He lived a solitary existence
And to himself did take no wife.
To be ever there for others,
The driven purpose of his life.

For the bereaved of this parish
He founded the widows' home
And his solicitude ensured
Their fate was not to be alone.

With the light skirts of the back streets
He spent much of his days
Dispensing of his counsel
For them to mend their ways.

His sensitivity of soul

Ensured all paths were taken
To console ladies in distress
Whom by their husbands were forsaken.

In penury he did die smiling,
Exhausted and alone.
(His thirty-seven children
Erected this headstone.)

PICK UP THE PIECES

Pick up the pieces
Shattered on the ground
And at your lonely table
Lay them down.
A veil of tears can only glorify
The way it had to end.
Pick up the pieces
Begin to mend.

Pick up the pieces
And given time
You may find that there are two
You can align
And you will feel this small success
Has taken you a while
But it will bring you
A fleeting smile.

Now other pieces
Fall into place
And slowly your momentum

Gathers pace,
Until you find as further pieces coincide,
You don't remember
When last you cried.

And with concession
To the sands of time
The final piece you fit
Will then consign
The past into the past, then look ahead to
What may come
And whisper softly
"What's done is done."

Pick up the pieces
And let it start,
The warm and gentle healing
Of your heart.
If every end has a beginning, find new beginning
At the end.
Pick up the pieces
Begin to mend.

WHEN YOU WERE VERY SMALL

I believed that your mother filled my heart.
No vacant space remained, she owned it all
But from the moment that the midwife introduced us,
My heart expanded when you were very small.

Your eyes were your first present from your mother
And you grew to have the same black gypsy hair
And when you giggled as I bounced you on my knee,
I discovered I had so much love to spare.

Soon I became the fount of all known wisdom,
A more than testing role to occupy
For I became your encyclopedia,
When a hundred times a day you would ask, "Why?"

You learned to count, thanks only to your

birthdays
For your birthday became your idea of heaven.
Each day you'd ask, "How many days now to my birthday?"
I would sigh and tell you one hundred and seven.

I would say, "Let's walk to town, I'll take the pushchair."
You'd say you'd walk, then I knew what was on the cards
For soon I'd hear, "Dad I'm tired will you please carry me?"
When we had only gone a hundred yards.

At bedtime,"The Wolf and Seven Little Kids"
Was the story I knew you'd pick from the start
And your brother would say, "Oh! No! Not again!"
Then I'd recite the whole thing off by heart.

On a day the rain was pouring down,
With the pavement being sprayed by passing trucks,
By the time we reached the park, I would be

sodden
But I had promised that today we'd feed the ducks.

Never was there such a loving child
Who could melt the frail defences that I had,
When you would put your arms around my knees
And look up to me and say, "I love you dad."

And there might be a howling wind outside
And through our window pane, the rain might fall
But there was always sunshine in our home
In the precious days when you were very small.

Then suddenly I looked to see a lovely woman.
Through a father's eyes, the fairest of them all,
Yet I had known that this would happen from the start,
When first I saw you, when you were very small.

The day will come when I will walk you down the aisle

To stand beside the young man of your choice
Then I will speak to no-one for a while
To try to hide the tremor in my voice.

For it is then that I must step out of the limelight
And I must tell myself to be aware,
A love that's true will never claim possession.
You were only given to my care.

I will pray that he will make you happy
And as the autumn leaves begin to fall,
I will turn the pages back to warm my heart
And I'll remember when you were very small.

WELCOME TO PURGATORY

Welcome to purgatory.
You have arrived now where
You are between two stools
And are neither here nor there.

Your stay might well be short,
Though we have a long-term precinct.
Some souls have been staying there
Since dinosaurs became extinct.

In terms of a colour chart,
Blacks and Whites went their chosen way
But you comprise the largest group
In many shades of grey.

So purgatory is overcrowded
And while that might be sad,
You brought it on yourselves
By being neither good nor bad.

You are not here to be happy.

Laughter is not allowed.
It is essential to look miserable
So you don't stand out from the crowd.

We have no golf or tennis courts,
No swimming pool or bar.
The only service that we offer
Is a hair-shirt bazaar.

All games are forbidden
To help the time pass by,
Such as scissors, paper, stones.
And that includes "I spy."

Smiling or chuckling is prohibited,
Regarded as regrettable
But to weep or gnash your teeth
Is totally acceptable.

Should you look across the crowd
And see a face both warm and tender,
Interaction is forbidden
With anyone of any gender.

It always rains in purgatory

But look not for umbrella stand,
And at permanent full volume
We have a Heavy Metal band.

Everyday at twelve
All congregate in the main hall,
Then midges, wasps and fleas
Will be released amongst you all.

Breakfast is rat goulash.
The lunchtime maggots are quite lively.
Dinner is roadkill burger
Garnished with poison ivy.

We may not reach your desired standards
But if truth to tell,
Compared to one alternative,
This is a five star hotel.

So to all of our new residents,
We welcome you today
We trust that you will find no comfort
And have a wretched stay.

IF I HAD A PENNY

If I had a penny
For each time I'd wished for a penny,
Then an awful lot of pennies would be mine
But I'd keep wishing for a penny
Remembering days I had not any
And then when I had many
I'd be fine.

Then skies would all be blue
And my daydreams would come true
And the air I breathe be ever sweet.
No more would I self deny
For I would find pennies could buy
Into those who have the world
Lie at their feet.

Then I would sail the seven seas
And live a life of ease
But I might not find it easy to forget
The lesson I once learned

Of the satisfaction earned
From a penny gained
By honest sweat.

And maybe then I would forget
So many people I had met
Who didn't have a penny to their name.
For I would move in higher courts
With no penny for their thoughts
Even though I once was
Just the same.

But I want not to be apart
From those who live in my heart
With a self importance
That will give no inch.
Having only what might please me
Or comfort me or ease me,
For life had meaning when I had
To penny-pinch.

So let me not wish for a penny
For they may get too many
Let me wipe penny ambition from my eyes,
For it's a probability

I'd be pound foolish as could be,
Instead of being poor
But penny-wise.

OLD ADVERSARIES

The man of faith has long regarded with suspicion
The findings of the scientific man.
Each time he found something new,
And insight of physics grew,
The man of faith held to his creed how life began.

For him, Genesis was not to be questioned
And Galileo and his ilk were persecuted
And with Darwin too,
His theory, Bible Belts withdrew
And to guard his faith, much would be refuted.

A Galilean once said, "Ye of little faith."
Why then did the man of faith not say,
"I do not question what you found,
Wonder's of God lie all around
And science will reveal them day by day."

Then the man of science duly did just that
And the source of all creation duly beckoned
And he tells us today
That he can truly say
That all came into being in one second.

And secretly, the man of faith now smiles
For both he and the man of science know
That further theories stall
To the most basic law of all
That nothing is created from zero.

But the man of science says, "I am not finished
For I will prove it either way sooner or later
Whether the world we see was meant
Or a freak accident,
And I will bow to you if it was your creator."

Then the man of faith slowly shakes his head
And says, "For you I must impose a bitter pill
For by my faith it is the truth
That you will not find the proof
For Him to verify would negate man's free will."

Why am I here and what made the world around

me?
Both science and religion ask in vain
But whatever or whether
They must journey on together
For old adversaries are searching for the same.

HE WHO KNOWS

He who knows not but knows not that he knows not,
Is regarded as being somewhat dim
But he who knows not and knows that he knows not
Is inclined to get along with him.

For both of them know not but only one knows
That he is the one who knows that he knows not
And he knows that he who knows not and knows not that he knows not,
Sadly doesn't know an awful lot.

He who knows but knows not that he knows
Has also found it to be true
That he who knows not and knows not that he knows not
Is unknowing that he hasn't got a clue.

Then he who knows not but knows that he

knows not
Sought he who knows and knows he knows
from reading books,
But found he who knows and knows he knows
quite haughty,
Much given to head shakes and knowing looks.

Then he who knows and knows he knows held
up his hand
And said, "I draw this meeting to a close
Those who know not cannot waste the time
Of such as I who knows and rightly knows he
knows."

Then he who knows not and knows that he
knows not
With tear-stained eyes sought comfort from his
friends
And he who knows not and knows not that he
knows not
Said, "I won't stand for this and I will make
amends."

Then he who knows not and knows not that he
knows not

Said to he who knows and knows he knows,
"now see,
If you hurt a friend of mine again
Then know you will be answering to me."

Then he who knows not that he knows and he who knows he doesn't know
Agreed to interchange the status quo,
For sometimes he who doesn't know and doesn't know he doesn't know
Is the better person to know.

ALL AS ONE

From where hails mercy,
A quality apart
That counsels clemency to callous heart?
That tells defeated foe
Who awaits to die or live
" I have taken,
I will now give."

What lends capacity
To empathise,
To feel the pain displayed in careworn eyes,
To bless the palm of he
Who has the least,
To dance most joyful
At the wedding feast?

Tender compassion
From where derives
Bringing compulsion to reach out to fragile lives,
To tend the ailing and ensure empty mouths are

fed,
To bring solicitude
To the stricken bed?

What motivation
Leads us to care,
To cling not to our blessings but to share,
To be generous in spirit and in deed,
To walk with angels
For those in need?

And yet these qualities
Are all as one,
They raise up man to the divine and they are sprung
From the noblest gift to which we have recourse,
They are love's children.
Love is the source.

ON THE FIRST DAY OF LENT

On the first day of Lent
My true love said to me
Give up watching football on TV.

On the second day of Lent
My true love said to me
Give up your daily paper,
And give up watching football on TV.

On the third day of Lent
My true love said to me
Give up going to the bookmaker,
Give up your daily paper,
And give up watching football on TV.

On the fourth day of Lent
My true love said to me
Give up sugar in your coffee and your tea,
Give up going to the bookmaker,
Give up your daily paper,
And give up watching football on TV.

On the fifth day of Lent
My true love said to me
Give up the malt whisky you take each night at ten,
Give up sugar in your coffee and your tea,
Give up going to the bookmaker,
Give up your daily paper,
And give up watching football on TV.

On the sixth day of Lent
My true love said to me
Give up going to the club to meet your friends,
Give up the malt whisky you take each night at ten,
Give up sugar in your coffee and your tea,
Give up going to the bookmaker,
Give up your daily paper,
And give up watching football on TV.

On the seventh day of Lent
My true love said to me
Give up cake, give up chocolate, give up chips,
Give up going to the club to meet your friends
Give up the malt whisky you take each night at ten,

Give up sugar in your coffee and your tea,
Give up going to the bookmaker,
Give up your daily paper,
And give up watching football on TV.

On the eighth day of Lent
My true love said to me
Give up your daily twenty-pack of filter tips,
Give up cake, give up chocolate, give up chips,
Give up going to the club to meet your friends,
Give up the malt whisky you take each night at ten,
Give up sugar in your coffee and your tea,
Give up going to the bookmaker,
Give up your daily paper,
And give up watching football on TV.

On Easter Sunday morning
I leapt out of bed.
I got back all I'd given up
And gave up my true love instead.

MORE OR LESS

Less spawns endeavour
Less motivates
Less finds a seed of strength within
That germinates.
Dormant talents overlooked are utilised,
Less forms a character
Unrealised.

Less opens eyes
Less lets us see
Of the challenge for so many
Life can be.
When the maintenance of less takes will and labour
Less teaches us
To help our neighbour.

Less can be hard
Less can be cruel
Yet less will lose its sting played for a fool

For with the gift of life bestowed
And given free
Less is the spur
To be what we might be.

More offers ease
More opens doors
More takes leave on distant
Sun-kissed shores.
Opportunities are given for the seizing,
More is addictive
More is self pleasing.

More dulls the senses
More's disposition
Is to draw the blueprint for
Next acquisition.
More can fail to countenance or guess
As to the daily toil of those
Who live with less.

More isolates
More is cocooned
More on his comfort desert island
Is marooned

And the irony that has crept in by stealth
Is he has made the best for him
But not the best of himself.

And should it be
Life is a test
And of ourselves we are enjoined
To make the best,
Then if overcoming trials of life
Contribute to our score,
Then more is less
And less is more.

GARDEN CENSOR

A leafy, suburban garden
Sounds like a pleasant place
But when you take a closer look
It's an absolute disgrace.
Birds are mating in full view.
Could they not wait till after dark?
I've even heard they sometimes do it
In a public park.

Take a look behind a bush
At twilight, noon or dawn
And you will be appalled
At what is really going on.
Cats take out birds, birds murder frogs,
Frogs kill snails and slugs,
Slugs terminate the plants
And bugs assassinate other bugs.

A greenfly lays a thousand babies
She has them by the score

Then when a wasp eats them alive
She simply lays a thousand more.
A furry, little caterpillar
Climbing a stem, arches his back
Unaware he's on the menu
For a blackbird snack.

Weeds spill a million seeds
Once their petals are unfurled
In their determination
To take over the world
And they grow overnight,
By morning they have a firm hold
To smother and to strangle
An innocent marigold.

A little field mouse takes a wander
Among the flower beds,
Then he is swooped on by a hawk
And he is torn to shreds,
And everything is fornicating
In pansies and in every shrub,
Sparrows, spiders, earwigs, slugs,
Think they're in a swingers' club.

So ban your children from the garden
For common decency and sense,
For the whole place is awash
With sex and violence.

HUMAN INTERRACTION

My doctor looked at me and said
"I'm really quite concerned
With your medical history
And all that I have learned.

You are on anti-depressants
And you say you wish you'd died
On last Christmas day
When you attempted suicide.

Now you tell me you talk to no-one
Every day and every week,
In fact it's only when you see me
That you're inclined to speak.

To withdraw in deep depression
Is a deadly curse,
You must have human interaction
Or it only will get worse.

To talk to people will uplift you.
At first, you might find it a strain
But just remark about the weather
Say, "I think it's going to rain."

So when you leave my surgery
And you walk down the street,
Engage in conversation
With the first person you meet."

So I walked out to the bus stop
Apprehensive as could be
And found there was another man
Standing next to me.

He looked a bit dishevelled
With an expression somewhat grim
But I summoned up my courage
And turned and spoke to him.

"It doesn't look too nice," I stammered,
"The clouds are darkening again,
I wouldn't be surprised
If it was going to rain."

He turned to stare at me
And he said, "Rain, do you say?
Get on your knees and you be thankful
If that's all you get today.

For we are at the end of days
The apocalypse is nigh,
At any moment you will see
The four horsemen in the sky.

They will bring conquest and disease,
Be ready to take your last breath.
They will bring war and famine
And for all a tortured death.

Then there will be the Last Judgement
When those who have failed to repent
Will be banished from his kingdom
And to the fires of hell be sent.

So I urge you wretched sinner
To repent in deadly fear,
You cannot say you were not warned
The end of the world is here."

I went back to tell the doctor
I'd interacted in the street,
But asked him, "Does it really have to be
The first person I meet?"

AFTER DELIVERY

"Do you think that there is life after delivery?"
In the womb, one baby asked his twin.
"Don't be so ridiculous, "said his brother,
"The only life we have is the one we're in."

"I'm inclined to think we have a mother,
Who nurtures us and keeps us in her care."
" Look around, there is no sign of a mother,
If we can't see her, then how can she be there?"

"But if I lie still and I keep very quiet,
I hear something that I cannot see,
The sound of a soft and loving voice,
And I think that she is speaking to me.

I think she knows that we are here and deeply cares,
That she loves us and wants for us to grow.
This cord of life we have is linked to her,
I can think that she is there but I can't know."

"Dear twin, you only fool yourself.
There is no mother, of that you may be sure.
This is all there is and all there will be,
After delivery, there will be nothing more."

"Please forgive me if I think you are mistaken
For you are very dear to me, my brother
But I am thinking there is life after delivery
And I look forward to the day I meet our mother."

LITTERBUG

They flip, they flop, they somersault and hop,
They indulge in pointless quest to catch their tails.
They climb up to me
Then fall off the settee,
This litter of two boys and two females.

This was never planned, this was underhand
But my house cat mum found an open door.
She met a cat of adverse gender
Happy to be a sex offender
And the subsequent results roll round my floor.

Now my life is not my own, neither is my home,
Each step I take akin to walking round land-mines.
Before I sit, I check my chair
To ensure no-one is there
When I forget, I hit the ceiling several times.

I did not ask for this. solitude is bliss,

I told them all today, "One thing is certain.
The proper place for you
Is probably a zoo."
They ignored me and promptly climbed the curtain.

I organised today, a kitten litter tray
And I told them all, "Go there....do as I bid!"
They blinked at me in mild rebuke,
As if they were saying, "Look....
We'll go anywhere we want." And so they did.

They may be amateurs but they are student saboteurs,
Fluffy demons with angelic faces,
And I have to bite my lip
When I stand up and trip
To find that they have undone my shoelaces.

I thought that I might watch a film tonight
But of the storyline I never could keep track,
For concentration disappears
When you have mountaineers
Climbing and abseiling on your back.

Tonight, one climbed on my knee as I watched TV
And a strange thing happened as I stroked his fur.
It didn't last for long
And I might have got it wrong
But I could have sworn I heard him purr.

At daybreak when I show, they all come to say, "Hello."
It's as if they're pleased to see me in the morning.
I kneel down with them on the rug.....
I have contracted litterbug!!.....
This is all becoming too heart warming.

Now when I sit on my own, I never am alone
For they have grown more trusting and much bolder.
One curls up close to me,
Two sit on my knee
And the daring boy is sleeping on my shoulder.

It's hard to know soon comes the day
When I must give them away.

Come that hour, I must stand straight and tall
But I can feel it in my bones,
I need to quickly find them homes
Or very soon I will decide to keep them all.

THE FAULT FINDING SOCIETY

The committee cast their votes
But the outcome now denies me
Of the role of chairperson
Of the Fault Finding Society.
Yet I have worked so long and hard
To bring our team success
But now they've selected Liz
With that so familiar dress.

Our events manager rambled on,
Some ladies think he cuts a dash
But I'm fairly sure Adonis
Did not have egg on his moustache.
Then Ken, the treasurer, took the floor
To drone about our bank account.
I added up his spots and pimples
Until I gave up the count.

The barman brought us lukewarm beers,
I said, "You call this a hotel?
This place is second only

To the Bates Motel."
The buffet was equally bad.
I'd rather chew some dry muesli
And I made them change the music
No one likes Elvis Presley.

They let Barbara take the minutes,
What a pointless caper.
It will look like a nest of spiders
Crawled across the paper.
Jim Scott finally arrived.
He always gets here late,
A hundred yards takes him an hour,
He's so grossly overweight.

They voted Norman for vice-chairman,
What a rock bottom choice,
He's got a lisp and rolls his "r"s,
Who wants to listen to that voice?
Vera Booth kept piping up,
She's just a trollop and a flirt.
She's never owned a high cut blouse
Or a knee length skirt.

When they confirmed the vote for Liz

I was downhearted and dejected.
I told her I sincerely hoped
She'd do better than I expected.
But at the close I was heart-warmed
With a final vote because
I was this year's outstanding member
And they gave me loud applause.

ADDICTION

Misguided in an hour of weakness
I took recourse to you,
Now I am constrained within your clutch.
There was a time I did not walk blindfolded
Once my path was true without your crutch.

But then I sought your comfort
To lose myself in you
And leave the world to take what course it may
But solace metamorphed into dependence
And dependence drew more needful every day.

To spend one day without you
Was to be more than alone
When reason for my heartbeat would be lost,
Then whatever it would take, I'd go to find you
And I would never stop to count the cost.

But no solutions did you offer,
Only the means to turn away
From the trials this life will daily send.

You gave oblivion to let the world bypass me
And Judas, I thought of you as my friend.

And to those I dearly love
I am diminished
And you are seen not as a friend but as a thief
For you have undermined all that I might have been
And you are the harbinger of grief.

And their tears have led my heart
To revelation
For somewhere in my soul a truth is found
That a true friend will raise you up to stand alone,
Not halt and lame, sustaining you in their debt bound.

You are the prince of dark deception
Portraying friend in need
Only to lessen all that I might do
And I will never know of my potential
When I give myself to lean on you.

Let me have will to find the key

To unlock my chains
Allow me strength for your false comfort to disown.
My faithless friend, this is the time to say goodbye.
Let me stand or fall but let me stand alone.

HAPPY WHATEVER

Thanks to the shops all bringing forward
The seasons of the year,
My family are somewhat muddled
With all the days of good cheer.

I bought Easter eggs at Christmas
And hid them in the garden so
The children could have an egg hunt
Digging up the snow.

On February fourteenth
All the family had a meeting
Then we put on our monster outfits
And went out Trick or Treating.

Fathers' Day was special,
The best one by a yard.
We had fireworks and a bonfire
And they gave me a New Year card.

Mum's birthday was a knock-out,
We gathered round the Christmas tree
Then we all sang Auld Lang Syne
And had hot cross buns for tea.

On November the fifth,
We couldn't let it pass,
We gave each other Valentines
And went to Midnight Mass.

Our shop tells us it's nearly Christmas.
They are so helpful and so good.
So in our sunglasses and shorts,
We bought turkey and Christmas pud.

I must praise our supermarket
And I say that because
How would we know without them,
What time of year it was?

METAMORPHOSIS

A metamorphosis occurs when a life alters
In such dramatic way to stun and to befuddle.
To offer you a sample,
Take a tadpole for example,
Which is a worm-like life form
Wriggling in a puddle.

Any still waters can in fact be its birthplace,
It may be a pond or stream or a damp bog.
Soon amongst its murky dregs,
It grows arms and it grows legs
Then appears upon the bank
A handsome frog.

A tiny speck that is scarce worth of notice,
The sort of trash that in a vacuum bag is found,
Is not worth a second look
But play it by the book
And be astounded when you put it
In the ground.

For it will metamorphose into small leaves
And within two years once it slowly grows,
It will abandon all pretences
And glorify the senses
With the scented, stunning beauty
Of a rose.

The little caterpillar with its arched back,
One day decides to make a parcel of itself.
He spins himself into a sheath,
Hanging on a leaf,
Then something wonderful is happening
By stealth.

For this apparent suicide is not the end,
A metamorphosis occurs as time goes by.
The cocoon soon sways and surges,
A thing of beauty then emerges,
A magnificently coloured butterfly.

How come the caterpillar, tadpole and the rose seed
All change into something so wonderful to be?
There should be legislature
To condemn mother nature

For her unkind metamorphosis
Of me.

Once I was young and I was strong and I was dashing,
I thought nothing of partying till dawn
But this idyll did not last
For as the decades passed
I turned into a relic
Hanging on.

Now my back ignores instructions from my brain,
My demeanour is a deep sigh and a frown.
I need glasses for my eyes.
Just waking up is a surprise,
And all the mirrors in my house
Are taken down.

Yet every form of life must accept change
For metamorphosis can clearly work each way,
But like the butterfly and rose,
The frog and all that grows,
Let me be thankful that I
Once had my day.

WITHOUT ADVERSITY

Given plain sailing,
No storms in wait
With an elementary course to navigate,
Then will the voyager know not how tides are turned,
Without adversity
Nothing is learned.

But in this ocean
High winds are rife,
Safe anchorage is fleeting in this life
And from the age of reason to the grave,
The only lifebuoys
Are for the brave.

It is ordained
For humankind
To encounter barriers that must be climbed
And they are not unique to only one,
For they are given

To everyone.

They are but hurdles
That we must leap,
For what we do not sow we cannot reap,
Yet those who clear the jump will gain the more
And will be stronger
Than once before.

A tribulation
Once overcome
Bestows resilience to deal with the next one
And character will grow with every test
And of man's nature
Will forge the best.

Then do not look
For easy course
Where the strength that lies within is dammed at source
For we may never be as much as we might be,
In still waters
Without adversity.

SO LAST CENTURY

"Dad, may I have a word?
Please don't get me wrong
But there are things I need to say
That I have held back for so long.

The kind of things you say and do
Have got me down of late.
Dad, I'm afraid you are old fashioned
And completely out of date.

My friends' dads have Lamborghinis
Some have sports cars even finer.
How do you think we feel
When you still drive a Morris Minor?

You keep saying, "Super"
Which is really quite absurd,
Everybody knows that "Awesome"
Is the appropriate word.

We really love you dad

But you just don't know where it's at.
How often have we asked you
To stop wearing a cravat?

You have no designer gear,
I can't believe you've no tattoos
And words completely fail me
About your blue suede shoes.

You don't like Heavy Metal
And for no reason I can see,
You think that Rap is awful.
Dad, you are so last century."

"Son, you may criticise me
But I have striven all my days
To keep up with changing fashions
And all the latest ways.

For you to say I am old fashioned
I must admit sticks in my throat
But to show I bear no grudge
Have this ten shilling note."

YOUR FELLOW SERVANT

Barely conscious, he lay in the roadside ditch
Where his body had been hurled by the impact,
Vaguely aware that blood was running down his face,
One hip was broken and several ribs were cracked.

One moment he was walking on the grass verge
Strolling into the setting sun,
Only to find that he was prone amongst the nettles,
The victim of a callous hit and run.

Now and then a car would speed on by
Then what frail hopes that he had left were further sunk.
Where he lay, he guessed that he was partly hidden
Or if noticed, had been dismissed as a drunk.

By now the pain was near beyond what he could bear
And the first shadows were diminishing the day.
As his cries for help were met with total silence,
In desperation he began to pray.

And he prayed thus, "God help me in my hour of need.
I am a Christian and I have been loyal to you.
In my despair, send me your fellow servant.
Night is falling and my chances growing few."

Suddenly, footsteps were running to his side
Where he lay semi-conscious as he prayed
And a voice said, "Friend, I am here to help you.
You will be safe now.
Allah be praised."

IT'S A BEAUTIFUL DAY

I will meet him every now and then
When he's well enough to take the morning air.
I will stop and he will talk of this and that
As he sits in his wheelchair.

Our conversations have told me much about him
He wears a colostomy bag at his waistband
And it has been four years since both of his legs
Lost their ability to stand.

His winning smile is eighty three years old
Yet still he loves to have his little joke,
He says he's looking forward to the anniversary
Of when he had his last stroke.

And I found that even cancer is no stranger.
For he was hospitalised only this last year
But he tells me that he's such a lucky man
For now he's been given the all-clear.

He says he lives alone but he likes company
And he said, "Any time you like come visit me."
I'm advised he lives at number forty seven
But I'll have to brew my own tea.

I spoke about him to a mutual neighbour
Who said that there was something that I did not know.
His wife was killed in a head- on car crash
And that was only seven months ago.

If the rain pours when next we meet, I'll stop to ask him
How he is, knowing what he will always say…
"If I awake each day and see the sun rise,
Then it's a beautiful day."

IT'S YOUR WORLD NOW

We were determined to set the world alight,
To be the force for change that could not wait.
Fortitude we did not lack
Yet when we look back
We leave a legacy unfit to advocate.

We meant to rid mankind of poverty and war,
From the rooftops we championed a better day
Then mortgages and family
Ambushed what we were meant to be
And we succumbed to live our lives in changeless way.

Now our yesterdays are drawing to a close
And we see our broken dreams as we look round.
Our failures were too many,
Victories were few, if any
For hate and persecution still abound.

It was our world and this is what we made of it.
So little change worthy of commendation.
Too many tears and so much grief
Too many wars, too little peace
We bequeath to you, next generation.

You are young as many years ago were we,
Impulsive, opinionated, loud and bold
But since the world began
Nature unfolds her constant plan
That the new will ever supersede the old.

Then put an end to injustice and hostility,
Self deny to fill your brother's empty plate,
Make peace that which you seek,
Lend your shoulder to the weak
And bring love to those who only know of hate.

It's your world now, our children, we leave it to you.
We stand in shadows while the fates allow.
We pray you are given grace
To make our world a better place.
Embrace it.
Make it so.

It's your world now.

AS YOU FIND THEM

There are nice people who come across as nice
But be sure to look them over once or twice,
For there are those to whom niceness you bequeath
Who really are quite nasty underneath.

Yet there are some who seem nasty through and through
But you may be surprised by nice things that they do,
For the nasty may have a nice quality
Which surprises the likes of you and me.

Totally nice people sometimes may be found
But they are fairly thin upon the ground
And in their company it is hard to give pause
To the constant search to find their flaws.

But with true nasty people there is nothing vague

And it is best that you avoid them like the plague.
Seek out nice people yet always bear in mind,
Even nice people can sometimes be unkind.

If nasty people sometimes may do something nice
And nice people may hide a secret vice,
Then when we appraise somebody new,
How may we construct a point of view?

Wicked villains and saints surely exist
But are not plentiful on nice or nasty list
So when you assess the nasty or nice riddle,
Be aware most folk are somewhere down the middle.

There will be those who offer whispers of the wise,
"They are nasty or they're nice," they will advise
But ignore them, pay no heed and do not mind them,
Just take other people as you find them.

SOMETHING WILL HAPPEN

Something will happen, be not surprised
When an ever changing world confronts our eyes.
We seek safe harbour but what we gain
Is not equipped
To stay the same.

Something will happen, for all things pass,
This fleeting breath of life made not to last.
We embrace the dreams fulfilled today
That sands of time
Will take away.

And when we chance upon a cup of joy,
We are free to drink of pleasure and enjoy
But we know full well that by and by
That cup will empty
And will run dry.

Human spirit also runs aground

Where there is no place to go but further down
But lives no millstone that will not shift,
Something will happen
That will uplift.

In our book of life the chapters re-arrange
With the story ever subject to a change
But when both happiness and grief linger awhile,
Treat them likewise
With knowing smile.

For we are fated to walk on shifting sand
And destiny obeys no man's command
But when we wake to winds of change with a new dawn
And something happens,
We must walk on.

HEDGEHOG CROSSING

A country lane tends to lose its charm
In a penguin feather wind and driving rain,
When passing cars will guarantee you saturation
Then attempts to raise one's spirits are in vain.

I glanced around me to confirm the only fool
Was me, out walking in this weather
But up ahead of me were two hooded teenagers
With their heads down, huddling together.

Then of a sudden, they ran out into the road
And for one moment I was at a loss
Then I saw that they were standing either side
Of a hedgehog who was trying to get across.

And they held up their hands to halt oncoming traffic
And pointed to the hedgehog's slow advance
And they shooed him on his way across the tarmac
And he hurried over while he had the chance.

Then as he disappeared into the hedgerow,
The teenagers hurried back to the roadside
And as they held their thumbs up to the traffic,
With smiles and tooting horns, the drivers all replied.

And the rain dwindled to a stop
Now mother nature had ordained there'd be no drought
And she painted a rainbow in the sky
And she smiled upon humanity
As the sun came out.

THE BANK NOTE

Freshly printed, newly minted,
I lay crisp and clean and new,
My life's journey to begin in a short while
And the image that I bore
Of a very special lady
In the darkness of the bank vault
Gave a smile.

Then I was packed, I was stacked
Into a vending machine
Then was withdrawn and placed upon a horse,
But my first owner left that place
Cursing and swearing
When his wager fell at the
Newmarket course.

Back at the bank, my spirits sank
When an old man took me out
And crumpled in a dirty pocket could scarce
breathe.

Then he spent all of me
Drinking alcohol
Until the barman told him that
He had to leave.

Then I was used, I was abused
For strange transactions
When for little packs of powder I was traded.
Soon the traces of this powder
Stuck to me
And I felt humiliated
And degraded.

And in such way, my everyday
Passed unrewarded,
Anticipation of my usefulness was gone
And every time there was an outbreak
Of a virus,
It would adhere to me and
I would pass it on.

And I grew old and I grew cold,
Crumpled and dirty,
No worthwhile purpose did I serve that I could see.

Very soon I'd be removed
From circulation,
The bank in my dishevelled state
Would withdraw me.

But then I flew where skies were blue
With man and wife
To where the sun shone brightly everyday.
One day they walked me through
A dusty market
Where many ragged children
Were at play.

Lost and beguiled, stood one small child
In deep devotion
Gazing longingly upon a market stall.
Many passed her by oblivious
And uncaring
Yet when my owners stopped, I knew
They saw it all.

They watched awhile then with a smile
That spoke of kindness,
They haggled with the trader that he might take less

Then price agreed, I was handed to the seller
And the little girl was given
The red dress.

With tearful face, they were embraced
And thanked profusely
And suddenly a bank note's life became
worthwhile
And the image I bore of
A special lady
In the trader's pocket
Gave a smile.

NO GOOD WILL

To my ex-wife Griselda
Whose fidelity I mistook,
I leave a list of all her lovers,
The local telephone book.

And to her lawyers, Grabb and Bankett,
Who kept her divorce claims on track,
I leave them what they left me,
The shirt upon my back.

For my accountant brother Vince
Who had control of my affairs,
I leave the penny that was left
When he fled to God knows where.

To my Aunt Amelia
Who never drank from loving cup,
I leave a witches' cauldron
So she can keep on stirring it up.

For my stepdaughter, Lola
Who gets out of jail next year
I leave her a pole
To resurrect her old career.

To my son George, who celebrated
Fathers Day with theft,
I bequeath the empty wallet
Which was all he kindly left.

Now as I lie on my sick bed
I can see the situation,
That this may be my last chance
To show them my appreciation.

So for my funeral reception
To ease their grief upon that day,
I paid for a hot air balloon
With a bar and a buffet.

With all the family aboard
They can raise their glasses high,
Toasting my loving memory
As they sail through the sky.

Now as I wait my final breath,
I am smiling at this juncture
For I can almost hear the hiss
Of air escaping from the puncture.

BITTER SWEET

A forgotten photograph falls on your table
From a treasured book he gave you long ago
And the picture plays a chord upon your heartstrings
And memories
Play melodies
That haunt you so.

And you are lost to see the lazy, laughing smile
And the look of love in warm and tender eyes.
So many treasured moments are awakened
That even now,
Some way, somehow
Still hold the power over you to hypnotise.

For he was the love who stole away your reason
And lifted you to heights unknown before,
Beyond all doubt you knew that it would last forever
Till left to cry,
He said goodbye

And closed the door.

Then every dawn invoked the need to face each day
And find a way to camouflage a broken heart
And the nights were set aside for endless grieving,
Spent all alone
Beside the phone
And when it failed to ring, the tears would start.

But passing time permitted heartache to diminish,
Now you have license to recall your time together
When there was an overflow of love and laughter,
Those joyful days
And loving ways
Will last forever.

Now you put the photograph back in the book
And bid the past affectionate retreat
But for a time the memories will linger,
Both good and bad

Happy and sad
And bitter sweet.

HOW DEEP A HEART

How deep a heart
How large or small
In self confinement
Or open to all?
No book may answer with a guarantee,
None can proclaim a heart's capacity.

Hearts will be broken.
Hearts will be scarred,
Then will those lives
Be spent on guard?
But too protected hearts may never know
How they may heal. How they may grow.

Shallow that heart
Should it then live
Blind to its command
That it must give,
Yet if it should be given a free rein
It resurrects and cares again.

For there are those
Who see no gain
In surrender to
A heartfelt pain,
Then as a pearl grown from an alien grain of sand,
That heart will flourish and will expand.

All beating hearts
Are uniform
Of an equal size
When we are born
But no limits can constrict a heart that's true,
How deep you fill your heart depends on you.

COLOUR CO-ORDINATION

God overheard his colours
Who he had just sent to earth,
Arguing with each other
About their respective worth.

Red said, "I'm brash, I'm loud,
I stand out and I impress,
When women wish to draw attention,
They will wear a red dress.
I'll be a mist, a warning light,
Cheeks of an embarrassed fool,
Never think you can upstage me
For that's a red rag to a bull."

Blue said, "I may be melancholy
But I am calm and I am cool,
I might have a blue aura
But I'm nobody's fool.
They'll sing to the moon about me,
They'll call me royal too

But if you try to put me down,
I will turn the air blue."

Violet said to Orange,
"At traffic lights, they all will know
That you are vague and indecisive
And are neither Stop nor Go."
Orange replied, "You think you're special
More like pathetic, I am thinking.
You'll be a tiny bashful flower
And they will call you shrinking."

Yellow said, "I just don't know
Why you think of me as the least,
I will be a mighty river
In the Far East.
I know I'll be the cowards' colour
Though I think that's rather mean
But one day they'll all sing about me
When I'm a submarine."

Green said, "You all are losers,
Behind your ears you all are green.
I surely am God's favourite colour
For everywhere I'm seen.

I'm in the grass, I'm in the flowers,
In the trees and forest scene.
I am Mother Nature's colour
Even in envy, you are green."

Then God scolded the colours
They surely knew that he was vexed.
He said, "Each one of you is lovely,
As equal as the next
But you must work in harmony
And from now on it will be so,
For every time it rains
You will make a rainbow."

THE PYSCHIATRIST

"Good morning, Mr. Sharp,
Please relax now if you would.
Let's begin with your childhood,
Could you say that it was good?"

"Yes, my childhood was first class,
I was happy all the time.
I guess that I was lucky.
Was yours as good as mine?"

"Mr. Sharp, that is not relevant,
This consultation's not interactive,
Now tell me about your mother,
Would you say she was attractive?"

"Dr. Woods, this is concerning,
You will not speak of your childhood,
Then you ask me such a question
Which most people would find rude."

"Mr. Sharp, let's speak of you

Or this will be of no good use.
Tell me about your father,
Perhaps you suffered some abuse."

"Certainly not, I had a father
Who was honest, good and true!
He was the perfect role model.
Was it not the same for you?

Now I'm concerned about your father,
Fixations with your mother too.
With questions such as this
I find I'm worrying about you."

"This consultation's not about me
Mr. Sharp, it's about you.
I need to hear some of your thoughts
To proceed with this interview."

"And you don't wear a wedding ring
As most men of your age do
But perhaps that's not surprising
With all that you've been through.

And looking over there,

I see you have a cat,
Preferring pets to deep relationships,
Is a revealing fact.

But you must not blame yourself
If your emotions have been blocked,
Let us live in hope
One day your heart will be unlocked."

"Mr. Sharp, I've had enough.
Please leave this room direct
Before I may do something
That I might regret."

"Doctor, I am not offended
With all that you've been through,
It is no surprise to me
You have anger management problems too.

So I am going to leave you now
Before you raise your fist
But be aware that you need help.
Please see a psychiatrist."

THE SHORT STRAW

Once the tunnel had been found, the die was cast,
Then they lined up at the Kommandant's command,
When he said it would be best
If those responsible confessed,
Each and every man put up his hand.

And his rage was something fearsome to behold
As he ironically applauded such display,
Then at random, there and then
He pulled out seven men
And gave them half an hour to choose which one would pay.

Then they were taken to a shed and were shut in
And all that they could do was sit and stare,
For each man's comrade was his brother
And they could not choose one another
And they became engulfed in dark despair.

One man then raised a fist enclosing seven straws
And said, "This is the only way this can be done.
We cannot choose who lives or dies,
Allow that lady luck decides
For the one who is selected will have drawn the shortest one."

Then they all nodded in a calm, reluctant silence
And the first man bravely pulled out a long straw,
Then number two to number five
Kept their hopes alive
Until the outstretched fist held but two more.

The young corporal was now left to make his choice
Knowing full well that one was right and one was wrong.
He ran his fingers through his hair
And said a silent prayer
And then he drew the last straw that was long.

Now they all stared at the last remaining man
Who still held the short straw firmly in his hand

But after a short while
He looked up with a smile
And said, "I think this is the way God may have planned.

For as you know, I am your chaplain and your priest
And there are likely none to grieve for me
But precious are your lives
For you have children and have wives
And I pray you see the day that you are free."

And as the guards took him away, he turned and said,
"Now I must go but let me say before I do,
Let your hearts be strong
And may your lives be long
For lady luck chose well to bypass men like you."

Distractedly the corporal picked up all the straws
As from outside the sound of gunfire salvo came.
He whispered then, "God give me strength,
All of these straws are the same length."
For luck had never been invited to play the short

straw game.

RECYCLED RIB

Adam asked if he might speak with God
And said, "You know your wish is always my command
But the companion that you have created for me,
I am finding somewhat hard to understand.

In many ways, I find her most delightful,
She is a thing of beauty to my eyes.
She looks similar to me, yet she is different
And everything she says and does, is a surprise.

You made me and I bow to you Almighty
But it has been just you and me now for so long.
Not once did I give you cause to reprimand me,
Now much of what I do, I'm told is wrong.

I am told I am not neat and am not tidy.
I do not rinse out my drinking cup.
I leave my blankets in a heap at morning sunrise,
I should shake them out and then should fold them up.

At the river she will stare into still waters.
It seems that she sees her reflection there
And she will turn her head from side to side
And spend so long combing her long hair.

In this garden, there are so many flowers
Which are left to grow for pleasure that they bring
But she picks them for her hair and makes a chain around her neck,
Why would she want to do such a thing?

And the tree house that I worked so hard to make,
It didn't take too long for her to say
That she had found a tree with a much better view
Across the meadow and would I start on it today.

Yet there are times that I am hugged and she will smile
But it soon changes from affection to rebuffing
And when I hurry to enquire what might be wrong,
Every time her answer will be, "Nothing".

Master, I give you so much thanks for my companion
But self composure and my peace of mind is gone."
God smiled and laid his hand on Adam's shoulder
And gently said, "Get used to it my son."

HUMBUG

Good evening sir, please stop a moment.
Now let me take a guess...
You've just come from a party,
That's why you're wearing fancy dress?

May I assume that is your vehicle,
It would appear to be a sleigh
Drawn by antlered animals
Illegally parked in the roadway.

Such usage of wild animals,
May I point out with tact
Is in direct contravention
Of the Wildlife Protection Act.

So far, you have two offences
Attributed to your name,
Now may I ask why you are trespassing
In this private lane?

You must make a delivery

Of this highly suspicious sack
To a child you've never met,
That's why you carry it on your back?

But sir, it is the dead of night,
Your front door knock would not be heard.
Humour me sir and explain
How you intend this sack transferred.

I could not have seen this coming...
This is like something from Walt Disney...
You mean to climb up on the roof
And drop this sack down the chimney?

So let me get this straight sir,
For I am finding this quite hard,
Your intention is to trespass
And create a fire hazard?

So, on top of illegal parking,
If I take this to the wire,
We have animal abuse and trespass
And intent to risk a fire.

I must ask you to accompany me,

To the station we must go.
I wish you Merry Christmas too
But please stop saying Ho! Ho! Ho!

I ALWAYS TRIED

There were things that I could do something about,
Provide an answer,
Work things out.
I was given means to think and to be strong
To problem solve,
To right the wrong.

This existence has laid challenge at my door
To try me out,
To test my core.
There were successes that application earned
But there were failures
And then I learned.

For I will never calm a raging sea
Or make hatred
Cease to be.
Within my restrictions, I must be reconciled,
I cannot raise

A lifeless child.

I would rail and weep for what I could not do
When a loved one
Needed me to,
For a man may only offer prayer and cry
When someone dear
Must say goodbye.

For there are boundaries imposed upon my soul.
Times I will fail
To reach a goal
Then what is asked of me is do all that I can.
I am not God.
I am a man.

I know now although my motives may commend,
I may not sway
How tears will end
And be helpless with the passing days
To view the theft
Of dark malaise.

Yet while heart beats, a minor role is mine to

play.
Let me give
While give I may
For should I see my brother lying there
Still have I strength
His weight to bear.

One day soon, I will be asked to state my case
Within my limits
I found in place
And I will give my only answer in hope not to be denied,
I always cared.
I always tried.

IF I CAN HELP

I pointed out that he was visibly receding,
It was becoming more apparent by the day
And for him to put that right
I suggested that he might
Begin to brush his hair the other way.

I noticed that he wore corduroy slacks often,
So I gently pointed out with friendly smile
That it had been many a year
Since they had been classy gear
And they were now considered out of style.

I intimated he might sell his four-wheel drive
For he didn't really need so big a car
And with the current cost of fuel,
Some might call him a fool
For its consumption wouldn't take him very far.

Every hour, he'd go out for a cigarette
And there were often times when he would smoke two.

I took him to one side
And said that many folk had died
And said, "If you don't stop, that could happen to you."

I said I was surprised last night to see his daughter
For her hair once had a soft and natural curl,
Now it was cut close to her head
And she had dyed it red
Which was a shame for she had been a pretty girl.

He spent several nights a week inside the local
But I am not a taker, I'm a giver
So I felt it was my place
To speak to him face to face
And warn him all about sclerosis of the liver.

At coffee break he took three teaspoonfuls of sugar.
I said he'd benefit from less sugar in his cup,
But I truly was amazed
When he looked up with his eyes glazed
And rudely said, "Do me a favour and shut up."

EMPTY HANDED

They combined devotion with their dedication
For more than a decade since the day they started
And their monument would pass the test of time
And still tower so long after he'd departed.

On the day that he exhaled his final breath,
Even as grief consumed his children and his wife,
They began the rituals pre-ordained
For his journey to the afterlife.

His body was prepared that it might last
According to the alchemy of old
Then he was laid into a gleaming casket
Of lapis lazuli, of silver and of gold.

In his imposing stone built mausoleum
Beside his casket, they stood many jars
Containing richest food and finest wines

To refresh him on his journey to the stars.

And they furnished the whole room with his possessions,
To all that had been his, they took full heed.
All that he had owned was not forgotten
Nothing was overlooked that he might need.

They left his robes, his jewellery, they left his sandals.
They left the regalia that he wore.
They left his chariot and his favourite board game.
They left his drinking cup and his weapons of war.

Then content that they had duly served their master,
They sealed the chamber and prayed with heartfelt cry
Entreating all their gods to guard him safely
On his voyage to join them in the sky.

Many centuries unfolded from that day
Till an explorer found the entrance in the sand

And what he saw when finally he reached the chamber
Struck him silent with no words at his command.

For his torch revealed a history of wonder,
All the treasures of a bygone race
And everything was just as they had left it
Standing in its four thousand year old place.

For he had gone upon his journey empty handed
A truth that past and present all should know,
For princes, kings and queens and even pharaohs
Cannot take it with them when they go.

WEAR IT WITH PRIDE

The spirit of the boy looks in the mirror
But in his looking glass, himself he fails to see
Yet mirrors ever speak the truth
And what once was a striking youth
Is now an old man returning scrutiny.

Then he considers the old man in the reflection
Who bears so many signs of wear and tear.
He counts the creases on his brow
And vaguely wonders how
He managed to lose so much of his hair.

He tries to smile the way he used to do
But charm erodes and his smile has lost its touch
And bright eyes he once did own
Have taken wing and flown,
Now his dull eyes seem to say they've seen too much.

He remembers when this face was so expressive.

He recalls when girls would look his way,
Yet within his heart he knows
That was so many years ago
Now each sunrise he gives thanks for a new day.

His gaze is fixed upon this familiar stranger
As a stray tear wanders down his cheek,
Then he projects his chin
And draws a deep breath in
And the reflection in the glass begins to speak.

"I see the traces of a hope that never died.
I see the scars of conflict that I won and lost.
I see the laughter lines
That were my light in darkest times
And I see wisdom that came at such a cost.

This is my face, it is the diary of my journey
None may halt the flow of time or tide
But these creases and these lines,
All that I am, clearly defines
Then I must wear it, but will wear it with pride."

YOUR CAPTAIN SPEAKING

Good afternoon, ladies and gentlemen
This is your captain, Nigel Wright.
I hope that you are comfortable
And enjoying your flight.

We are cruising at an altitude
Of thirty thousand feet
But are encountering mild turbulence
So please stay in your seat.

This turbulence is not from headwinds,
That's not what it's about
But from an engine on our port wing
Which has suddenly cut out.

But flying with one engine short,
Pilots are trained to have the knack
And the percentage is quite high
Of the planes that make it back.

So please retain your seats

And sit back and relax
Although we have another problem
To complicate the facts.

You recall hurricane Belinda
Which swept across the USA,
I'm told it has veered off its course
And is directly in our way.

We cannot fly around it
For its vast size is mitigating
And we have insufficient fuel
Which is somewhat irritating.

So we must fly through its centre
Not an option I would choose
For it might be slightly bumpy
But please relax and have a snooze.

Now the turbulence is severe
And we are being tossed around
But let us all be thankful
No other engine has shut down.

Well! Would you believe it?

That's what I get for tempting fate!
I must advise our ETA
Is getting somewhat late.

The cabin crew would serve you drinks
But if you look carefully around
It is beyond their capabilities
When we are flying upside down.

I must observe this has not been
The most stable and restful flight.
We may land sooner than we think
For rapidly we're losing height.

But I must thank you for choosing
To travel with this airline
And we hope you will fly with us
Upon another time.

When you boarded, you were given
A detailed questionnaire slip,
Please tell us any faults you found
And what was best about your trip.

We have an old airline tradition

Which would be a shame to miss
To say the Lord's prayer in unison
At a time like this.

And to all of our passengers
I bid a heartfelt salute
But for now you must excuse me
While I put on my parachute.

FLOOD ALERT

Father, I must speak with you,
This project borders on insane,
You must know how seldom
In our country, we have rain.
No-one has more respect
For your piety and devotion
But I find it hard to visualise
Our homeland as an ocean.

Yet now we have a massive ark
Which work took many a day
And the carpenters and builders
Are looking for their pay,
So soon the family will be paupers,
Our cupboard will be bare
But you employed a hundred men
To capture animals by the pair.

And merchants now are bringing us
Creatures from lands far away.

We got two pandas and two sloths
And two koala bears today.
We caged all of the beasts
Not thinking they would procreate.
We started with two rabbits
And now there's thirty-eight.

We had to separate the elephants
And their collective weight divide
For when we kept them together
The ark tipped on its side
And we should not have taken beavers,
I doubt the ark will stay afloat
For it is made of wood
And they keep chewing up the boat.

To save the dodos from extinction,
The plan for their survival fails
If it is as I suspect
That we have got two females.
So stands an ark in burning sun
With no change in the weather.
The family is exhausted
And at the end of our tether.

I know you say you spoke with angels,
Who said this is what you must do
But everyone in town is laughing
And making fun of you.
Perhaps the course that you have taken
Was not what God did mean
Or maybe it did not happen
And it was just your dream.

You've worked your fingers to the bone
Of that there is no doubt
But now is the time to end this
And let all the animals out.............
But as I look through the window,
Perhaps I must think again……..
Father, I beg you for forgiveness
For it has begun to rain.

JUST AS GREEN

There are gargoyles glaring down from the main entrance.
There are turrets reaching to the sky.
Greek god statuary
Hide in the shrubbery
And there's a dovecote where silver pigeons fly.

In the pond, golden koi laze in the sun,
Rambling red roses scramble up many a trellis
And I chance to see
Beyond a monkey puzzle tree
A court, enquiring, "Anyone for tennis."

So many windows draped in silk damask curtains.
So many sunflowers to open on a sunlit morn,
And in emerald grace
With not one blade out of place
Unfolds the carpet of a perfect lawn.

As I walk past the country manor back to town,
A question lingers with each step I take,
How grand might it be
To live in such luxury
And stroll the perfect lawn with each daybreak?

Then I see my cat awaits me at my window,
I see the welcome sign above my door.
Neighbours who I know
With passing smiles call out, "Hello"
And I wonder why I'd ever wish for more.

I stand awhile and view my humble dwelling.
I see my patch of grass displays no verdant sheen
Perhaps unmanicured, unmown
But this is where I call home
And I realise my grass is just as green.

MISSING STETHOSCOPE

"This is how it was for me,
There comes one moment when you know
That you cannot endure the pain
And you must let go.
And letting go was such relief.
The agony had ended,
I drifted from my body
To the ceiling I ascended.

And looking down, I watched you striving
With your dedicated team
To bring me back to life
And my heartbeat to redeem.
I was calm, I was serene
With total clarity of sight
But I was so tempted to fly
To a warm and loving light.

Then time ceased to exist
As the thought entered my head

How can I overview
And hear every word that's said?
Now I was of a mind to leave
There was somewhere I'd rather be
But I was suddenly brought up short
When I thought of my family.

If I now had the choice,
How could I cause them so much pain?
Then I saw you punch the air
And I drew breath again.
So that is how it was for me
Those three days ago
Since it was you who brought me back,
I thought you'd like to know."

"With a doctor's inbred caution
I think I can now safely say
That you are past the worst
And are recovering each day.
Your out of body experience
Is really nothing new,
There have been similar descriptions
From previous patients too.

Once the human heart has failed
The brain does not have long
Until all oxygen is used
And then life is truly gone.
It cannot use the body's senses
For they have taken flight,
In fact the first sense to be lost
Is the sense of sight.

So the brain is blind and trapped
In panic and confusion,
If patients say they see and hear
That is merely an illusion
And it has nowhere to turn
In helpless degeneration
All it may now access
Is its own imagination.

Last thoughts of family may occur
That cannot be in doubt
But the warm and beckoning light
Is just the last light going out.
So for those who run this course
All may seem spiritual and mystic
But from my medical point of view

It is purely scientific."

"Doctor, I can only tell you
Of how it was for me
But of course I can accept
That you see it differently.
But please tell Nurse O'Connell
The scope that she's been looking for
Is above the surgical cupboard.
No-one can see it from the floor."

FAMILY TREE

One day, Ernie Flotsam Junior
Wondered about his family tree
And decided there and then
To research his ancestry.

First he checked his bottom drawer
Where special papers he did log
But found only old gas bills
And a photo of his dog.

Then he thought he'd pay a visit
To his local registrar
But she was much too busy
So he didn't get too far

Then he went to the nearest graveyard
And for days upon his own
He checked out each engraving
On every old gravestone.

But no epitaph he found there

That offered him a clue,
Then he became depressed
And wondered what next he might do.

So he went to the local church
Perhaps the vicar could give names
But they had had a recent fire
Where records had gone up in flames.

But then he had a brainwave
As he left the church
And he enrolled in a web-site
Who said that they'd do the research.

And at last he made the breakthrough
With all the data they did gather
And found that Ernie Flotsam Senior
Who lived upstairs was his father.

PRAYER FOR THE DEPARTED

Should your final breath have led you to a place
Exempt from grief and sickness and despair,
Where ecstasy is total and eternal
And those who shared your heart are waiting
there.

Where choirs of angels oh, so sweetly sing
Where love and only love exists each day
And this joy is not for now but is forever,
All of this for you, I humbly pray.

But when your eyes declined to see as heartbeat
ended,
Did you discover a place of uncertainty
Where sadness was to be your close companion
For just out of reach was where you wished to
be?

Then you must spend this time in deep reflection
For penitence will surely end your stay

And know your welcome is postponed but is not cancelled
And for your quick release, I humbly pray.

And I pray that if your final footsteps took you
To a fiery place of torment underground,
You found a notice blaming God's unending mercy,
That told you "Due to lack of guests, we are closed down."

HEN OR EGG?

It's crystal clear that the hen must have come first
In the question we have asked since way back when,
For any fool can see
It's an impossibility
To conjure up an egg without a hen.

But then, perhaps I need to think this through again
For this may be a can of worms I've stumbled on.
Just when I thought I'd worked it out
I have got a nagging doubt
For I am thinking now where did the hen come from?

Of course, the hen was hatched out of an egg
But this riddle has too many twists and turns
For suddenly I've realised
The egg had to be fertilised.

Now I have another can of worms.

For the egg to hold the embryo of a hen,
A rooster must have played a prior part
So logic then asserts
That the rooster was there first
But how come that he was there from the start?

And the answer is that he came from an egg
But let me pause for now a question begs…
For him to procreate
He would need a mate,
In the beginning then there must have been two eggs.

So then the whole thing must have started with two eggs.
I think I may have worked it out, but then…….
I can see a hitch,
My theory has a glitch
For how can you have two eggs without a hen?

So I think that I must think this through again
Then I am sure that I will come up with something.

But for now I'll turn my mind
To matters of another kind
While I consider how long is a piece of string.

THE HYPOCHONDRIOLOGIST

"I have an appointment,"
I told the receptionist,
"With Dr. David Fielding,
The Hypochondriologist."

"He will see you now,
He is just back from the health centre,
He awaits you Mr. Wilting,
Knock on his surgery door and enter."

"Good morning, Mr. Wilting.
My goodness, you look tired and grey.
I really have to tell you
You don't look well today."

"Thank you so much doctor,
At last someone can see
How sick and ill I am
Unlike my G.P.

My G.P. is useless

He's getting worse as he gets old,
When I went down with pneumonia
He said it was a cold.

Then when I caught bird flu,
He just said drink lots of fluids.
I had to fight it on my own,
I'd been as well consulting druids.

When I had a raging headache,
At the surgery, I called in
But when I asked him for a brain scan
He gave me aspirin.

He said I had neuralgia
When it was clearly meningitis
And when I had diphtheria
He called it tonsillitis."

"Excuse me, Mr. Wilting,
Permit me to interpose,
It seems to me you've been unlucky,
Consistently misdiagnosed.

So Mr. Wilting, I can see

The reasons for your consternation,
Now please remove your clothes
For a thorough examination...

I have completed every test
Now let me put you at your ease,
You are a walking corpse
And are infested with disease.

And when you leave my surgery
It may be you feel bereft
But try to make the best of
The few days you have left."

"Doctor, how can I ever thank you?
I am close to joyful tears.
I always told them I was ill,
This is the best I've felt in years."

PASSING STRANGERS

Bound by time, we come, we go
How long our stay, we cannot know.
Time dictates tomorrows always come
Yet one tomorrow
We will be gone.

This life is measured by passing years,
To laugh a while, to shed our tears
But the sands of time in stone are firmly cast.
I am but mortal
I will not last.

Do the stars exist today
Whose image came from far away?
For to the speed of light, time is the host
Do I behold then
A distant ghost?

Sun will arise, then take repose.
Time, we are subject to each moment you

impose.
Seeming pedestrian, but you are fleet,
For I walk with dinosaurs
Beneath my feet.

I have been told, could I but fly
Beyond the speed of light into the sky
To then return upon a distant day,
I would be younger than
When I flew away.

You are my gaoler, you are my master
For it is ordained that I might not fly faster.
You tightly hold the key to my earthly chain.
I am your servant
In your domain.

Yet come the hour, it will then be
Mortality offers me the key.
To all of life you are the great arranger
But you and I, time,
Are passing strangers.

THE CUSTOMER IS ALWAYS RIGHT

The customer is always right.
He or she is never wrong.
This maxim of the catering trade
Has been upheld for so long.

Yet on a Saturday night,
Short-staffed, pushed to the limit,
Patient customers are a blessing.
But there's one born every minute.

Instead of waiting at reception,
He pushed in through the door
And sat at the one vacant table,
A table laid for four.

I hurried over and said, "Sir,
Four customers can sit here."
It was as if I hadn't spoken.
He said, "Bring menu and a beer."

I then struggled to remember

The customer is never wrong.
I thought the quicker that I served him
The sooner he'd be gone.

So I rushed back with beer and menu
But it was no surprise to me
That he did not have a thank-you
In his vocabulary.

Then I attended other tables,
The service backlog plain to see.
I was beginning to catch up
When he shouted out to me.

"Hey, fella! Get a move on.
Get your ass over here.
I'm ready now to order
And fetch me another beer."

I went over and I asked him,
"Would you care for a starter, sir?"
He said, "Naw, I'll just have a main course.
Bring me a sole meuniere."

And it didn't take him long,

As I served another group
He shouted out, "I've changed my mind.
Just fetch me the soup."

Then as I hurried by his table
Too late, I saw his outstretched boot
And I tumbled my full length
As he withdrew his foot.

And I lay there feeling dizzy
As my head began to throb
And he looked down with a grin,
"Is that you sleeping on the job?"

So when I came back to his table,
He looked at me in doubt
As I held up the bowl of soup
And we stared each other out.

He said, "You'd love to pour that over me"
And leaned back in his chair.
He sneered, "You haven't got the nerve,
Go on….you wouldn't dare!"

Then the applause and commendations

Lasted through the night
Once one patron had discovered
The customer is not always right.

FORGIVENESS

Be wary as to that which you embrace,
For as Greeks with Trojan horse found to their woe,
There are many things that we should cling to
And likewise, there are those we must let go.
He who knows not what should be released
May think that what he holds brings comfort to his soul
But if what he clasps to his chest
Is drawn from a viper's nest,
Such misplaced solace will take of him its toll.

For there are few will lead this life without betrayal
Leaving a hurt as deep as any gaping wound
But if hatred then encompasses his heart,
From its saving bounty, he is then marooned.
For then he will drink in of the viper's poison
And strange to say a paradox is there to see,
For as hatred takes its cost
The victim then has lost

And he bequeaths the perpetrator a double victory.

For when our trust lies broken on the ground,
Only two paths may we then choose as how to live.
Embracing hatred and revenge, we are diminished
But are released should we elect that we forgive.
Then to our pain we do not add self harm
And we discover we were stronger than we thought.
Forgiveness has unchained our soul
And to absolve has made us whole
Then we will find the peace of mind so dearly sought.

FATAL ACCIDENT

"Mrs. Sedgewick, I am sad to hear your news
That from your much loved husband you are now bereaved.
May I offer you our sincere condolences
On behalf of undertakers "Grieve & Grieve."

With regard to the final arrangements,
Rest assured none of your wishes will be missed
And to that end we note specifications
Which you have detailed very clearly on this list.

To be certain your instructions are all followed
Appropriately as you would have us do,
Allow me to check over your requirements
And verify each mandate with you.

A normal casket is mahogany or oak
But nowadays of course it's costly to buy wood
And in your list you've written very clearly
That the coffin is to be made of plywood.

And you wish only one wreath upon the casket,
Not of lilies or of roses you've decreed,
Instead you have firmly indicated
That this wreath be made of Japanese knotweed.

The service pamphlet heading is, "Gone and Forgotten."
The normal hymn to be replaced with a refrain
Where you ask that all the mourners will sing loudly
To your choice of "Happy Days Are Here Again."

You are dispensing with the need to have a hearse
For you say here that you will hire a skip
Which will take the coffin and all his belongings
To the funeral service at the local tip.

Then in this hour when you are overcome with grief,
Be assured your wishes we will expiate.
All that remains is for me to ask you
Could you provide me with the death

certificate?"

"I'm afraid that for the moment I don't have it
But now I know what's being going on with her,
When he walks through this door tomorrow,
A fatal accident I'm certain will occur."

MULTITUDE OF GREYS

Grey in prominence.
Grey of shade,
Unremarkable, with no extreme displayed,
Comprising a silent multitude
Not steeped in evil, nor saintly good.

They are not black.
They are not white,
Will take the wrong path, then try to do what's right.
Then they will pray. Then they will curse.
They are not better. They are not worse.

They are strong.
They are weak,
Prone to addictive pleasures that they seek.
Yet if an ailing neighbour is struck down,
They will rally and gather round.

They wear no halo.

They wear no veil.
They will not stoop to those beyond the pale.
With life's temptations, they are beguiled
But never will they kill, nor harm a child.

Grey of hope.
Grey of belief,
Disillusioned by a world of grief.
Only human, yet even so, they try
But a blemished soul will be theirs when they die.

They are you.
They are me,
Who fail to be as much as we might be.
Good resolutions are fated to deflate
When yet another pitfall lies in wait.

Yet who may judge
The world of greys?
Unworthy of condemnation or of praise,
But surely He who strolled the lakeside acted not upon a whim
When twelve grey men were asked to follow Him.

Let me take heed
As best I can,
To never call myself the better man.
If I am to be judged at end of days,
Permit I take my stance among the greys.

Michael Dickson is a native of Edinburgh, Scotland but has lived in the picturesque town of Moffat for twenty years. He has two sons and a daughter (and two rag doll cats).

<u>Email</u>

michaelgdickson@yahoo.co.uk

Also by this author,

<u>Mountains and Molehills</u>

<u>On Second Thoughts</u>

available from Amazon

Printed in Great Britain
by Amazon